Separation from the World

By John Charles (J. C.) Ryle

ISBN-13: 978-1611045499

Published in 2011 by:

Waymark Books
P. O. Box 7
Cedar Lake, Michigan

http://www.waymarkbooks.com/

THE WORLD

"Come out from among them, and be ye separate, saith the Lord." 2 Cor. 6:17.

The text which heads this page touches a subject of vast importance in religion. That subject is the great duty of separation from the world. This is the point which Paul had in view when he wrote to the Corinthians, "Come out,—be separate."

The subject is one which demands the best attention of all who profess and call themselves Christians. In every age of the Church separation from the world has always been one of the grand evidences of a work of grace in the heart. He that has been really born of the Spirit, and made a new creature in Christ Jesus, has always endeavored to "come out from the world," and live a separate life. They who have only had the name of Christian, without the reality, have always refused to "come out and be separate" from the world.

The subject perhaps was never more important than it is at the present day. There is a widely-spread desire to make things pleasant in religion,—to saw off the corners and edges of the cross, and to avoid, as far as possible, self-deniaL On every side we hear professing Christians declaring loudly that we must not be "narrow and exclusive," and that there is no harm in many things which the holiest saints of old thought bad for their souls.

That we may go anywhere, and do anything, and spend our time in anything, and read anything, and keep any company, and plunge into anything, and all the while may be very good Christians,—this, this is the maxim of thousands. In a day like this I think it good to raise a warning voice, and invite attention to the teaching of God's Word. It is written in that Word, "Come out, and be separate."

There are four points which I shall try to show my readers, in examining this mighty subject.

I. First, I shall try to show *that the world is a source of great danger to the soul...*

II. Secondly, I shall try to show *what is not meant by separation from the world.*

III. Thirdly, I shall try to show in *what real separation from the world consists.*

IV. Fourthly, I shall try *to show the secret of victory over the world.*

And now, before I go a single step further, let me warn every reader of this book that he will never understand this subject unless he first understands what a true Christian is. If you are one of those unhappy people who think everybody is a Christian who goes to a place of worship, no matter how he lives, or what he believes, I

J. C. Ryle

fear you will care little about separation from the world.

But if you read your Bible, and are in earnest about your soul, you will know that there are two classes of Christians,—converted and unconverted. You will know that what the Jews were among the nations under the Old Testament, this the true Christian is meant to be under the New.

You will understand what I mean when I say that true Christians are meant, in like manner, to be a "peculiar people" under the Gospel, and that there must be a difference between believers and unbelievers. To you, therefore, I make a special appeal this day. While many avoid the subject of separation from the world, and many positively hate it, and many are puzzled by it, give me your attention while I try to show you "the thing as it is."

I. First of all, let me show that *the world is a source of great danger to the soul.*

By "the world," be it remembered, I do not mean the material world on the face of which we are living and moving. He that pretends to say that anything which God has created in the heavens above, or the earth beneath, is in itself harmful to man's soul, says that which is unreasonable and absurd. On the contrary, the sun, moon, and stars,—the mountains, the valleys, and the plains,—the seas, lakes, and rivers,—the animal and vegetable creation,—all are in themselves "very good." (Gen. 1:31.) All are full of lessons of God's wisdom and power, and all proclaim daily, "The hand that made us is divine." The idea that "matter" is in itself sinful and corrupt is a foolish heresy.

When I speak of "the world" in this book, I mean those people who think only, or chiefly, of this world's things, and neglect the world to come,—the people who are always thinking more of earth than of heaven, more of time than of eternity, more of the body than of the soul, more of pleasing man than of pleasing God. It is of them and their ways, habits, customs, opinions, practices, tastes, aims, spirit, and tone, that I am speaking when I speak of "the world." This is the world from which Paul tells us to "Come out and be separate."

Now that "the world," in this sense, is an enemy to the soul, the well-known Church Catechism teaches us at its very beginning. It tells us that there are three things which a baptized Christian is bound to renounce and give up, and three enemies which he ought to fight with and resist. These three are the flesh, the devil, and "the world."

All three are terrible foes, and all three must be overcome if we would be saved.

But, whatever men please to think about the Catechism, we shall do well to turn to the testimony of Holy Scripture. If the texts I am about to quote do not prove that the world is a source of danger to the soul, there is no meaning in words.

(a) Let us hear what Paul says:—

"Be not conformed to this world: but be ye transformed by the renewing of your mind." (Rom. 12: 2.)

"We have received, not the spirit of the world, but the Spirit which is of God." (1 Cor. 2:12.)

"Christ gave Himself for us, that He might deliver us from this present evil world." (Gal. 1:4.)

"In time past ye walked according to the course of this world." (Eph. 2:2.)

"Demas hath forsaken me, having loved this present world." (2 Tim. 4:10.)

(b) Let us hear what James says:—

"Pure religion and undefiled before God and the Father is this, To visit the fatherless and widows in their affliction, and to keep himself unspotted from the world." (James 1:27.)

"Know ye not that the friendship of the world is enmity with God? Whosoever therefore will be a friend of the world is the enemy of God." (James 4:4.)

(c) Let us hear what John says:—

"Love not the world, neither the things that are in the world. If any man love the world, the love of the Father is not in him. For all that is in the world, the lust of the flesh, and the lust of the eyes, and the pride of life, is not of the Father, but is of the world. And the world passeth away, and the lust thereof; but he that doeth the will of God abideth forever." (1 John 2:15-17.)

"The world knoweth us not, because it knew Him not." (1 John 3:1.)

"They are of the world: therefore speak they of the world, and the world heareth them." (1 John 4:5.)

"Whatsoever is born of God overcometh the world." (1 John 5:4.)

"We know that we are of God and the whole world lieth in wickedness." (1 John 5:19.)

(d) Let Us hear, lastly, what the Lord Jesus Christ:

"The cares of this world choke the Word, and it becometh unfruitful." (Matt. 13:22.)

"Ye are of this world: I am not of this world." (John 8:23.)

J. C. Ryle

"The Spirit of truth; whom the world cannot receive, because it seeth Him not, neither knoweth Him." (John 14:17.)

"If the world hate you, ye know that it hated Me before it hated you." (John 15:18.)

"If ye were of the world, the world would love his own: but because ye are not of the world, but I have chosen you out of the world, therefore the world hateth you." (John 15:19.)

"In the world ye shall have tribulation: but be of good cheer; I have overcome the world." (John 16:33.)

"They are not of the world, even as I am not of the world." (John 17: 16.)

I make no comment on these twenty-one texts. They speak for themselves. If anyone can read them carefully, and fail to see that "the world" is an enemy to the Christian's

Separation from the World

soul, and that there is an utter opposition between the friendship of the world and the friendship of Christ, he is past the reach of argument, and it is waste of time to reason with him. To my eyes they contain a lesson as clear as the sun at noon day.

I turn from Scripture to matters of fact and experience.

I appeal to any old Christian who keeps his eyes open, and knows what is going on in the Churches, I ask him whether it be not true that nothing damages the cause of religion so much as "the world"? It is not open sin, or open unbelief, which robs Christ of His professing servants, so much as the love of the world, the fear of the world, the cares of the world, the business of the world, the money of the world, the pleasures of the world, and the desire to keep in with the world. This is the great rock on which thousands of young people are continually making shipwreck. They do not object to any article of the Christian faith. They do not deliberately choose evil, and openly rebel against God, They hope somehow to get to heaven at last; and they think it proper to have some religion. But they cannot give up their idol: they must have the world. And so after running well and bidding fair for heaven, while boys and girls, they turn aside when they become men and women, and go down the broad way which leads to destruction. They begin with Abraham and Moses, and end with Demas and Lots wife.

The last day alone will prove how many souls "the world" has slain. Hundreds will be found to have been trained in religious families, and to have known the Gospel from their very childhood, and yet missed heaven. They left the harbour of home with bright prospects, and launched forth on the ocean of life with a father's blessing and a mother's prayers, and then got out of the right course through the seductions of the world, and ended their voyage in shallows and in misery. It is a sorrowful story to tell; but, alas, it is only too common! I cannot wonder that Paul says, "Come out and be separate."

II. Let me now try to show *what does not constitute separation from the world.*

The point is one which requires clearing up. There are many mistakes made about it. You will sometimes see sincere and well-meaning Christians doing things which God never intended them to do, in the matter of separation from the world, and honestly believing that they are in the path of duty. Their mistakes often do great harm. They give occasion to the wicked to ridicule all religion, and supply them with an excuse for having none. They cause the way of truth to be evil spoken of, and add to the offence of the cross. I think it a plain duty to make a few remarks on the subject. We must never forget that it is possible to be very much in earnest, and to think we are "doing God service," when in reality we are making some great mistake. There is such a thing as "zeal not according to knowledge." (John

Separation from the World

16:2; Rom. 10:2.) There are few things about which it is so important to pray for a right judgment and sanctified common sense, as about separation from the world.

(a) When Paul said, "Come out and be separate," he did not mean that Christians ought to give up all worldly callings, trades, professions, and business. He did not forbid men to be soldiers, sailors, lawyers, doctors, merchants, bankers, shop-keepers, or tradesmen. There is not a word in the New Testament to justify such a line of conduct. Cornelius the centurion, Luke the physician, Zenas the lawyer, are examples to the contrary. Idleness is in itself a sin. A lawful calling is a remedy against temptation. "If any man will not work, neither shall he eat." (2 Thess. 3:10.) To give up any business of life, which is not necessarily sinful, to the wicked and the devil, from fear of getting harm from it, is lazy, cowardly conduct. The right plan is to carry our religion into our business, and not to give up business under the specious pretense that it interferes with our religion.

(b) When Paul said, "Come out and be separate" he did not mean that Christians ought to decline all intercourse with unconverted people, and refuse to go into their society. There is no warrant for such conduct in the New Testament. Our Lord and His disciples did not refuse to go to a marriage feast, or to sit at meat at a Pharisee's table. Paul does not say, "If any of them that believe not bid you to a feast," you must not go, but only tells us how to behave if we do go. (1 Cor. 10:27.)

Moreover, it is a dangerous thing to begin judging people too closely, and settling who are converted and who are not, and what society is godly and what ungodly. We are sure to make mistakes. Above all, such a course of life would cut us off from many opportunities of doing good.

If we carry our Master with us wherever we go, who can tell but we may" save some," and get no harm? (1 Cor. 9:22.)

(c) When Paul says, "Come out and be separate," he did not mean that Christians ought to take no interest in anything on earth except religion. To neglect science, art, literature, and politics,—to read nothing which is not directly spiritual,—to know nothing about what is going; on among mankind, and never to look at a news chapter,—to care nothing about the government of one's country, and to be utterly indifferent as to the persons who guide its counsels and make its laws,—all this may seem very right and proper in the eyes of some people. But I take leave to think that it is an idle, selfish neglect of duty.

Paul knew the value of good government, as one of the main helps to our "living a quiet and peaceable life in godliness and honesty." (1 Tim. 2:2.) Paul was not ashamed to read heathen writers, and to quote their words in his speeches and writings. Paul did not think it beneath him to show an acquaintance with the laws and customs and callings of the world, in the illustrations he gave from them. Christians who plume themselves on their ignorance of secular things are precisely the Christians who bring religion into contempt. I knew the case of a blacksmith who would not come to hear his clergyman preach the Gospel, until he found out that be knew the properties of iron. Then he came.

(d) When Paul said, "Come out and be separate," he did not mean that Christians should be singular, eccentric, and peculiar in their dress, manners, demeanor, and voice. Anything which attracts notice in these matters is most objectionable, and ought to be carefully avoided. To wear clothes of such a color, or made in such a fashion, that when you go into company every eye is fixed on you, and you are the object of general observation, is an enormous mistake. It gives occasion to the wicked to ridicule religion, and looks self-righteous and affected. There is not the slightest proof that our Lord and His apostles, and Priscilla, and Persis, and their companions, did not dress and behave just like others in their own ranks of life. On the other hand, one of the many charges our Lord brings against the Pharisees was that of "making broad their phylacteries, and enlarging the borders of their garments," so as to be "seen of men." (Matt, 23:5.) True sanctity and sanctimoniousness are entirely different things. Those who try to show their unworldliness by wearing conspicuously ugly clothes, or by speaking in a whining, snuffling voice, or by affecting an unnatural slavishness, humility, and gravity of manner, miss their mark altogether, and only give occasion to the enemies of the Lord to blaspheme.

(e) When Paul said, "Come out and be separate," he did not mean that Christians ought to retire from the company of mankind, and shut themselves up in solitude.

It is one of the crying errors of the Church of Rome to suppose that eminent holiness is to be attained by such practices. It is the unhappy delusion of the whole army of monks, nuns, and hermits. Separation of this kind is not according to the mind of Christ. He says distinctly in His last prayer, "I pray not that Thou shouldest take them out of the world, but that Thou shouldest keep them from the evil." (John 17:15.) There is not a word in the Acts or Epistles to recommend such a separation. True believers are always represented as mixing in the world, doing their duty in it, and glorifying God by patience, meekness, purity, and courage in their several positions, and not by cowardly desertion of them. Moreover, it is foolish to suppose that we can keep the world and the devil out of our hearts by going into holes and corners. True religion and unworldliness are best seen, not in timidly forsaking the post which God has allotted to us, but in manfully standing our ground, and showing the power of grace to overcome evil.

(f) Last, but not least, when Paul said, "Come out and be separate," he did not mean that Christians ought to withdraw from every church in which there are unconverted members, or to refuse to worship in company with any who are not believers, or to keep away from the Lord's table if any ungodly people go up to it.

This is a very common but a very grievous mistake. There is not a text in the New Testament to justify it, and it ought to be condemned as a pure invention of man. Our Lord Jesus Christ Himself deliberately allowed Judas Iscariot to be an apostle for three years, and gave him the Lord's Supper. He has taught us, in the parable of the wheat and tares, that converted and unconverted will be "together till the harvest," and cannot be divided. (Matt. 13:30.) In His Epistles to the Seven Churches, and in all Paul's Epistles, we often see faults and corruptions mentioned and reproved; but we are never told that they justify desertion of the assembly, or neglect of ordinances. In short, we must not look for a perfect Church, a perfect congregation, and a perfect company of communicants, until the marriage supper of the Lamb. If others are unworthy churchmen, or unworthy partakers of the Lord's Supper, the sin is theirs and not ours: we are not their judges. But to separate ourselves from Church assemblies, and deprive ourselves of Christian ordinances, because others use them unworthily, is to take up a foolish, unreasonable, and unscriptural position. It is not the mind of Christ, and it certainly is not Paul's idea of separation from the world.

I commend these six points to the calm consideration of all who wish to understand

Separation from the World

the subject of separation from the world. About each and all of them far more might be said than I have space to say in this chapter.

About each and all of them I have seen so many mistakes made, and so much misery and unhappiness caused by those mistakes, that I want to put Christians on their guard. I want them not to take up positions hastily, in the zeal of their first love, which they will afterwards be obliged to give up.

I leave this part of my subject with two pieces of advice, which I offer especially to young Christians.

I advise them, for one thing, if they really desire to come out from the world, to remember that the shortest path is not always the path of duty. To quarrel with all our unconverted relatives, to "cut" all our old friends, to withdraw entirely from mixed society, to live an exclusive life, to give up every act of courtesy and civility in order that we may devote ourselves to the direct work of Christ,—all this may seem very right, and may satisfy our consciences and save us trouble. But I venture a doubt whether it is not often a selfish, lazy, self-pleasing line of conduct, and whether the true cross and true line of duty may not be to deny ourselves, and adopt a very different course of action.

I advise them, for another thing, if they want to come out from the world, to watch against a sour, morose, ungenial, gloomy, unpleasant, bearish demeanor, and never to forget that there is such a thing as "winning without the Word." (1 Peter 3:1.) Let them strive to show unconverted people that their principles, whatever may be thought of them, make them cheerful, amiable, good-tempered, unselfish, considerate for others, and ready to take an interest in everything that is innocent and of good report. In short, let there be no needless separation between us and the world. In many things, as I shall soon show, we must be separate; but let us take care that it is separation of the right sort. If the world is offended by such separation we cannot help it. But let us never give the world occasion to say that our separation is foolish, senseless, ridiculous, unreasonable, uncharitable, and unscriptural.

III. In the third place, I shall try to show *what true separation from the world really is.*

I take up this branch of my subject with a very deep sense of its difficulty. That there is a certain line of conduct which all true Christians ought to pursue with respect to "the world, and the things of the world," is very evident. The texts already quoted make that plain.

The key to the solution of that question lies in the word "separation." But in what separation consists it is not easy to show. On some points it is not hard to lay down particular rules; on others it is impossible to do more than state general principles, and leave everyone to apply them according to his position in life. This is what I shall now attempt to do.

(a) First and foremost, he that desires to "come out from the world, and be separate," *must steadily and habitually refuse to be guided by the world's standard of right and wrong.*

The rule of the bulk of mankind is to go with the stream, to do as others, to follow the fashion, to keep in with the common opinion, and to set your watch by the town-clock. The true Christian will never be content with such a rule as that. He will simply ask, What saith the Scripture? What is written in the Word of God?

He will maintain firmly that nothing can be right which God says is wrong, and that the customs and opinions of his neighbors can never make that to be a trifle which God calls serious, or that to be no sin which God calls sin. He will never think lightly of such sins as drinking, swearing, gambling, lying, cheating, swindling, or breach of the seventh commandment, because they are common, and many say, "Where is the mighty harm?"

That miserable argument,—"Everybody thinks so, everybody says so, everybody does it, everybody will be there,"—goes for nothing with him. Is it condemned or approved by the Bible? That is his only question. If he stands alone in the parish, or town, or congregation, he will not go against the Bible. If he has to come out from the crowd, and take a position by himself, he will not flinch from it rather than disobey the Bible. This is genuine Scriptural separation.

(b) He that desires to "come out from the world and be separate," *must be very careful how he spends his leisure time.*

This is a point which at first sight appears of little importance. But the longer I live, the more I am persuaded that it deserves most serious attention. Honorable occupation and lawful business are a great safeguard to the soul, and the time that is spent upon them is comparatively the time of our least danger.

Separation from the World

The devil finds it hard to get a hearing from a busy man. But when the day's work is over, and the time of leisure arrives, then comes the hour of temptation.

I do not hesitate to warn every man who wants to live a Christian life, to be very careful how he spends his evenings. Evening is the time when we are naturally disposed to unbend after the labors of the day; and evening is the time when the Christian is too often tempted to lay aside his armour, and consequently brings trouble on his soul. "Then cometh the devil, and with the devil the world. Evening is the time when the poor man is tempted to go to the public-house, and fall into sin.

Evening is the time when the tradesman too often goes to the Inn parlour, and sits for hours hearing and seeing things which do him no good. Evening is the time which the higher classes choose for dancing, card playing, and the like; and consequently never get to bed till late at night. If we love our souls, and would not become worldly, let us mind how we spend our evenings. Tell me how a man spends his evenings, and I can generally tell what his character is.

The true Christian will do well to make it a settled rule never to *waste* his evenings. Whatever others may do, let him resolve always to make time for quiet, calm thought,—for Bible-reading and prayer. The rule will prove a hard one to keep. It may bring on him the charge of being unsocial and over strict. Let him not mind this. Anything of this kind is better than habitual late hours in company, hurried prayers, slovenly Bible reading, and a bad conscience. Even if he stands alone in his parish or town let him not depart from his rule. He will find himself in a minority, and be thought a peculiar man. But this is genuine Scriptural separation.

(c) He that desires to "come out from the world and be separate," must *steadily and habitually determine not to be swallowed up and absorbed in the business of the world.*

Separation from the World

A true Christian will strive to do his duty in whatever station or position he finds himself, and to do it well.

Whether statesman, or merchant or banker, or lawyer, or doctor, or tradesman, or farmer, he will try to do his work so that no one can find occasion for fault in him. But he will not allow it to get between him and Christ. If he finds his business beginning to eat up his Sabbaths, his Bible-reading, his private prayer, and to bring clouds between him and heaven, he will say, "Stand back! There is a limit. Hitherto thou mayest go, but no further. I cannot sell my soul for place, fame, or gold." Like Daniel, he will make time for his communion with God, whatever the cost may be. Like Havelock, he will deny himself anything rather than lose his Bible-reading and his prayers. In all this he will find he stands almost alone. Many will laugh at him, and tell him they get on well enough without being so strict and particular. He will heed it not. He will resolutely hold the world at arm's length, whatever present loss or sacrifice it may seem to entail. He will choose rather to be less rich and prosperous in this world, than not to prosper about his soul. To stand alone in this way, to run counter to the ways of others, requires immense self-denial. But this is genuine Scriptural separation.

(d) He that desires to "come out from the world and be separate" must steadily *abstain from all amusements and recreations which are inseparably connected with sin.*

This is a hard subject to handle, and I approach it with pain. But I do not think I should be faithful to Christ, and faithful to my office as a minister, if I did not speak very plainly about it, in considering such a matter as separation from the world.

Let me, then, say honestly, that I cannot understand how anyone who makes any pretense to real vital religion can allow

Separation from the World

himself to attend races and theatres. Conscience, no doubt, is a strange thing, and every man must judge for himself and use his liberty. One man sees no harm in things which another regards with abhorrence as evil. I can only give my own opinion for what it is worth, and entreat my readers to consider seriously what I say.

That to look at horses running at full speed is in itself perfectly harmless, no sensible man will pretend to deny.

That many plays, such as Shakespeare's, are among the finest productions of the human intellect, is equally undeniable. But all this is beside the question. The question is whether horse-racing and theatres, as they are now conducted, in England, are not inseparably bound up with things that are downright wicked. I assert without hesitation that they are so bound up. I assert that the breach of God's commandments so invariably accompanies the race and the play, that you cannot go to the amusement without helping sin.

I entreat all professing Christians to remember this, and to take heed what they do. I warn them plainly that they have no right to shut their eyes to facts which every intelligent person knows, for the mere pleasure of seeing a horse-race, or listening to good actors or actresses. I warn them that they must not talk of separation from the world, if they can lend their sanction to amusements which are invariably connected with gambling, betting, drunkenness, and fornication. These are the things "which God will judge."—"The end of these things is death." (Heb. 13:4; Rom. 6:21.)

Hard words these, no doubt! But are they not true?

It may seem to your relatives and friends very strait-laced, strict, and narrow, if you tell them you cannot go to the races or the theatre with them. But we must fall back on first principles. Is the world a danger to the soul, or is it not? Are we to come out from the world; or are we not? These are questions which can only be answered in

Separation from the World

one way. If we love our souls we must have nothing to do with amusements which are bound up with sin. Nothing short of this can be called genuine scriptural separation from the world.**

(e) He that desires to "come out from the world, and be separate," must be *moderate in the use of lawful and innocent recreations.*

No sensible Christian will ever think of condemning all recreations. In a world of wear and tear like that we live in, occasional unbending and relaxation are good for all. Body and mind alike require seasons of lighter occupation, and opportunities of letting off high spirits, and especially when they are young. Exercise itself is a positive necessity for the preservation of mental and bodily health. I see no harm in cricket, rowing, running, and other manly athletic recreations. I find no fault with those who play at chess and such-like games of skill.

We are all fearfully and wonderfully made. No wonder the poet says,—

*"Strange that a harp of thousand strings
Should keep in tune so long."*

Anything which strengthens nerves, and brain, and digestion, and lungs, and muscles, and makes us more fit for Christ's work, so long as it is not in itself sinful, is a blessing, and ought to be thankfully used. Anything which will occasionally divert our thoughts from their usual grinding channel, in a healthy manner, is a good and not an evil.

But it is the excess of these innocent things which a true Christian must watch against, if he wants to be separate from the world. He must not devote his whole heart, and soul, and mind, and strength, and time to them, as many do, if he wishes to serve Christ. There are hundreds of lawful things which are good in moderation, but bad when taken in excess: healthful medicine in small quantities,—downright poison when

Separation from the World

swallowed down in huge doses. In nothing is this so true as it is in the matter of recreations. The use of them is one thing, and the abuse of them is another. The Christian who uses them must know when to stop, and how to say "Hold: enough!"—Do they interfere with his private religion?

Do they take up too much of his thoughts and attention?

Have they a secularizing effect on his soul? Have they a tendency to pull him down to earth? Then let him hold hard and take care. All this will require courage, self-denial, and firmness. It is a line of conduct which will often bring on us the ridicule and contempt of those who know not what moderation is, and who spend their lives in making trifles serious things and serious things trifles.

But if we mean to come out from the world we must not mind this. We must be "temperate" even in lawful things, whatever others may think of us. This is genuine Scriptural separation.

(f) Last, but not least, he that desires to "come out from the world and be separate "must be *careful how he allows himself in friendships, intimacies, and close relationships with worldly people.*

We cannot help meeting many unconverted people as long as we live. We cannot avoid having intercourse with them, and doing business with them, unless "we go out of the world." (1 Cor. 5:10.) To treat them with the utmost courtesy, kindness, and charity, whenever we do meet them, is a positive duty. But acquaintance is one thing, and intimate friendship is quite another. To seek their society without cause, to choose their company, to cultivate intimacy with them, is very dangerous to the soul.

Human nature is so constituted that we cannot be much with other people without effect on our own character.

The old proverb will never fail to prove true: "Tell me with whom a man chooses to live, and I will tell you what he is." The

Separation from the World

Scripture says expressly, "He that walketh with wise men shall be wise; but a companion of fools shall be destroyed." (Prov. 13:20.) If then a Christian, who desires to live consistently, chooses for his friends those who either do not care for their souls, or the Bible, or God, or Christ, or holiness, or regard them as of secondary importance, it seems to me impossible for him to prosper in his religion. He will soon find that their ways are not his ways, nor their thoughts his thoughts, nor their tastes his tastes; and that, unless they change, he must give up intimacy with them. In short, there must be separation. Of course such separation will be painful.

But if we have to choose between the loss of a friend and the injury of our souls, there ought to be no doubt in our minds. If friends will not walk in the narrow way with us, we must not walk in the broad way to please them.

But let us distinctly understand that to attempt to keep up close intimacy between a converted and an unconverted person, if both are consistent with their natures, is to attempt an impossibility.

The principle here laid down ought to be carefully remembered by all unmarried Christians in the choice of a husband or wife. I fear it is too often entirely forgotten.

Too many seem to think of everything except religion in choosing a partner for life, or to suppose that it will come somehow as a matter of course. Yet when a praying, Bible-reading, God-fearing, Christ-loving, Sabbath-keeping Christian marries a person who takes no interest whatever in serious religion, what can the result be but injury to the Christian, or immense unhappiness? Health is not infectious, but disease is. As a general rule, in such cases, the good go down to the level of the bad, and the bad do not come up to the level of the good. The subject is a delicate one, and I do not care to dwell upon it. But this I say confidently to every unmarried Christian man or woman,— if you love your soul, if you do not want to

Separation from the World

fall away and backslide, if you do not want to destroy your own peace and comfort for life, resolve never to marry any person who is not a thorough Christian, whatever the resolution may cost you. You had better die than marry an unbeliever. Stand to this resolution, and let no one ever persuade you out of it. Depart from this resolution, and you will find it almost impossible to "come out and be separate." You will find you have tied a millstone round your own neck in running the race towards heaven; and, if saved at last, it will be "so as by fire." (1 Cor. 3:15.)

I offer these six general hints to all who wish to follow Paul's advice, and to come out from the world and be separate. In giving them, I lay no claim to infallibility; but I believe they deserve consideration and attention.

I do not forget that the subject is full of difficulties, and that scores of doubtful cases are continually arising in a Christian's course, in which it is very hard to say what is the path of duty, and how to behave. Perhaps the following bits of advice may be found useful.—In all doubtful cases we should first pray for wisdom and sound judgment. If prayer is worth anything, it must be specially valuable when we desire to do right, but do not see our way.—In all doubtful cases let us often try our selves by recollecting the eye of God. Should I go to such and such a place, or do such and such a thing, if I really thought God was looking at me?—In all doubtful cases let us never forget the second advent of Christ and the day of judgment. Should I like to be found in such and such company, or employed in such and such ways?

Finally, in all doubtful cases let us find out what the conduct of the holiest and best Christians has been under similar circumstances. If we do not clearly see our own way, we need not be ashamed to follow good examples. I throw out these suggestions for the use of all who are in difficulties about disputable points in the matter of separation from the world. I cannot help thinking that they may help to untie many knots, and solve many problems.

IV. I shall now conclude the whole subject by trying to *show the secrets of real victory over the world.*

To come out from the world of course is not an easy thing. It cannot be easy so long as human nature is what it is, and a busy devil is always near us. It requires a constant struggle and exertion; it entails incessant conflict and self-denial; it often places us in exact opposition to members of our own families, to relations and neighbors; it sometimes obliges us to do things which give great offence, and bring on us ridicule and petty persecution. It is precisely this which makes many hang back and shrink from decided religion. They know they are not right; they know that they are not so "thorough" in Christ's service as they ought to be, and they feel uncomfortable and ill at ease. But the fear of man keeps them back. And so they linger on through life with

Separation from the World

aching, dissatisfied hearts,—with too much religion to be happy in the world, and too much of the world to be happy in their religion. I fear this is a very common case, if the truth were known.

Yet there are some in every age who seem to get the victory over the world. They come out decidedly from its ways, and are unmistakably separate. They are independent of its opinions, and unshaken by its opposition.

They move on like planets in an orbit of their own, and seem to rise equally above the world's smiles and frowns..

And what are the secrets of their victory? I will set them down.

(a) The first secret of victory over the world is a *right heart*.

By that I mean a heart renewed, changed and sanctified by the Holy Spirit,—a heart in which Christ dwells, a heart in which old things have passed away, and all things become new. The grand mark of such a heart is the bias of its tastes and affections. The owner of such a heart no longer likes the world, and the things of the world, and therefore finds it no trial or sacrifice to give them up. He has no longer any appetite for the company, the conversation, the amusements, the occupations, the books which he once loved, and to "come out" from them seems natural to him. Great indeed is the expulsive power of a new principle! Just as the new spring-buds in a beech hedge push off the old leaves and make them quietly fall to the ground, so does the new part of a believer invariably affect his tastes and likings, and make him drop many things which he once loved and lived in, because he now likes them no more. Let him that wants to "come out from the world and be separate," make sure first and foremost that he has got a new heart. If the heart is really right, everything else will be right in time.

"If thine eye be single, thy whole body shall be full of light." (Matt. 6:22.) If the affections are not right, there never will be right action.

(b) The second secret of victory over the world is a *lively practical faith* in unseen things.

What saith the Scripture? "This is the victory that overcometh the world, even our faith." (1 John 5:4.) To attain and keep up the habit of looking steadily at invisible things, as if they were visible,—to set before our minds every day, as grand realities, our souls, God, Christ, heaven, hell, judgment; eternity,—to cherish an abiding conviction that what we do not see is just as real as what we do see, and ten thousand times more important,—this, this is one way to be conquerors over the world. This was the faith which made the noble army of saints, described in the eleventh chapter of Hebrews, obtain such a glorious testimony from 'the Holy Spirit. They all acted under a firm persuasion that they had a real God, a real Savior, and a real home in heaven, though unseen by mortal eyes. Armed with this faith, a man regards this world as a shadow compared to the world to come, and cares little for its praise or blame, its enmity or its rewards. Let him that wants to come out from the world and be separate, but shrinks and hangs back for fear of the things seen, pray and strive to have this faith. "All things are possible to him that believes." (Mark 9:23.) Like Moses, he will find it possible to forsake Egypt, seeing Him that is invisible.

Like Moses, he will not care what he loses and who is displeased, because he sees afar off, like one looking through a telescope, a substantial recompense of reward. (Heb. 11:26.)

(c) The third and last secret of victory over the world is to attain and cultivate the *habit of boldly confessing Christ* on all proper occasions.

In saying this I would not be mistaken. I want no one to blow a trumpet before him, and thrust his religion on others at all seasons.

But I do wish to encourage all who strive to come out from the world to show their colors, and to act and speak out like men who are not ashamed to serve Christ. A steady, quiet assertion of our own principles, as Christians,—an habitual readiness to let the children of the world see that we are guided by other rules than they are, and do not mean to swerve from them,—a calm, firm, courteous maintenance of our own standard of things in every company,—all this will insensibly form a habit within us, and make it comparatively easy to be a separate man.

It will be hard at first, no doubt, and cost us many a struggle; but the longer we go on, the easier will it be.

Repeated acts of confessing Christ will produce habits.

Habits once formed will produce a settled character. Our characters once known, we shall be saved much trouble.

Men will know what to expect from us, and will count it no strange thing if they see us living the lives of separate peculiar people. He that grasps the nettle most firmly will always be less hurt than the man who touches it with a trembling hand. It is a great thing to be able to say "No" decidedly, but courteously, when asked to do anything which conscience says is wrong. He that shows his colors boldly from the first, and is never ashamed to let men see "whose he is and whom he serves," will soon find that he has overcome the world and will be let alone. Bold confession is a long step towards victory.

It only remains for me now to conclude the whole subject with a few short words of application. The danger of the world ruining the soul, the nature of true separation from

Separation from the World

the world, the secrets of victory over the world, are all before the reader of this chapter. I now ask him to give me his attention for the last time, while I try to say something directly for his personal benefit.

(1) My first word shall be *a question.* Are you overcoming the world, or are you overcome by it?

Do you know what it is to come out from the world and be separate, or are you yet entangled by it, and conformed to it? If you have any desire to be saved, I entreat you to answer this question.

If you know nothing of "separation," I warn you affectionately that your soul is in great danger. The world passeth away; and they who cling to the world, and think only of the world, will pass away with it to everlasting ruin. Awake to know your peril before it be too late.

Awake and flee from the wrath to come. The time is short. The end of all things is at hand. The shadow are lengthening. The sun is going down. The night cometh when no man can work. The great white throne will soon be set. The judgment will begin. The books will be opened. Awake, and come out from the world while it is called to-day.

Yet a little while, and there will be no more worldly occupations and worldly amusements,—no more getting money and spending money,—no more eating, and drinking, and feasting, and dressing, and ball-going, and theatres, and races, and cards, and gambling. What will you do when all these things have passed away forever? How can you possibly be happy in an eternal heaven, where holiness is all in all, and worldliness has no place? Oh, consider these things, and be wise! Awake, and break the chains which the world has thrown around you.

Awake, and flee from the wrath to come.

Separation from the World

(2) My second word shall be *a counsel*.

If you want to come out from the world, but know not what to do, take the advice which I give you this day. Begin by applying direct, as a penitent sinner, to our Lord Jesus Christ, and put your case in His hands. Pour out your heart before Him. Tell Him your whole story, and keep nothing back. Tell Him that you are a sinner wanting to be saved from the world, the flesh, and the devil, and entreat Him to save you.

That blessed Savior "gave Himself for us that He might deliver us from this present evil world." (Gal. 1:2.)

He knows what the world is, for He lived in it thirty and three years. He knows what the difficulties of a man are, for He was made man for our sakes, and dwelt among men. High in heaven, at the right hand of God, He is able to save to the uttermost all who come to God by Him,—able to keep us from the evil of the world while we are still living in it,—able to give us power to become the sons of God,—able to keep us from falling,—able to make us more than conquerors. Once more I say, Go direct to Christ with the prayer of faith, and put yourself wholly and unreservedly in His hands. Hard as it may seem to you now to come out from the world and be separate, you shall find that with Jesus nothing is impossible. You, even you, shall overcome the world.

(3) My third and last word shall be *encouragement*.

If you have learned by experience what it is to come out from the world, I can only say to you, Take comfort, and persevere. You are in the right road; you have no cause to be afraid. The everlasting hills are in sight. Your salvation is nearer than when you believed. Take comfort and press on.

. No doubt you have had many a battle, and made many a false step. You have sometimes felt ready to faint, and been half-

Separation from the World

disposed to go back to Egypt. But your Master has never entirely left you, and He will never suffer you to be tempted above that you are able to bear. Then persevere steadily in your separation from the world, and never be ashamed of standing alone. Settle it firmly in your mind that the most decided Christians are always the happiest, and remember that no one ever said at the end of his course that he had been too holy, and lived too near to God.

Hear, last of all, what is written in the Scriptures of truth:

"Whosoever shall confess Me before men, him shall the Son of man also confess before the angels of God." (Luke 12: 8.)

"There is no man that hath left house, or brethren, or sisters, or father, or mother, or wife, or children, or lands, for my sake, and the gospel's, But he shall receive an hundred-fold now in this time, houses, and brethren, and sisters, and mothers, and children, and lands, with persecutions; and

J. C. Ryle

in the world to come eternal life." (Mark 10:29, 30.)

"Cast not away therefore your confidence, which hath great recompense of reward. For ye have need of patience, that, after ye have done the will of God, ye might receive the promise. For yet a little while, and He that shall come will come, and will not tarry." (Heb. 10:35-37.)

Those words were written and spoken for our sakes.

Let us lay hold on them, and never forget them, Let us persevere to the end, and never be ashamed of coming out from the world, and being separate. We may be sure it brings its own reward.

**NOTE.

Thoughtful and intelligent readers will probably observe that, under the head of worldly amusements, I have said nothing about ball-going and card-playing. They are delicate and difficult subjects, and many classes of society are not touched by them. But I am quite willing to give my opinion, and the more so because I do not speak of them without experience in the days of my youth.

(a) Concerning ball-going, I only ask Christians to judge the amusement by its tendencies and accompaniments. To say there is anything morally wrong in the mere bodily act of dancing would be absurd.

David danced before the ark. Solomon said, "There is a time to dance." (Eccl. 3:4.) Just as it is natural to lambs and kittens to frisk about, so it seems natural to young people, all over the world, to jump about to a lively tune of music. If dancing were taken up for mere exercise, if dancing took place at early hours, and men only danced with men, and women with women, it would be needless and absurd to object to it. But everybody knows that this is not what is meant by modern ball-going. This is an amusement which involves very late hours, extravagant dressing, and an immense amount of frivolity, vanity, jealousy, unhealthy excitement, and vain conversation. Who would like to be found in a modern ball-room when the Lord Jesus Christ comes the second time? Who that has taken much part in balls, as I myself once did, before I knew better, can deny that they have a most dissipating effect on the mind, like opium-eating and dram-drinking on the body? I cannot withhold my opinion that ball-going is one of those worldly amusements which "war against the soul," and which it is wisest and best to give up. And as for those parents who urge their sons and daughters, against their wills and inclinations, to go to balls, I can only say that they are taking on themselves a most dangerous responsibility, and risking great injury to their children's souls.

(b) Concerning card-playing, my judgment is much the same. I ask Christian people to try it by its tendencies and

Separation from the World

consequences. Of course it would be nonsense to say there is positive wickedness in an innocent game of cards, for diversion, and not for money. I have known instances of old people of lethargic and infirm habit of body, unable to work or read, to whom cards in an evening were really useful, to keep them from drowsiness, and preserve their health. But it is vain to shut our eyes to facts. If masters and mistresses once begin to play, cards in the parlour, servants are likely to play cards in the kitchen; and then comes in a whole train of evils. Moreover, from simple card-playing to desperate gambling there is but a chain of steps. If parents teach young people that there is no harm in the first step, they must never be surprised if they go on to the last.

I give this opinion with much diffidence. I lay no claim to infallibility.

Let everyone be persuaded in his own mind. But, considering all things, it is my deliberate judgment that the Christian who wishes to keep his soul right, and to "come out from the world," will do wisely to have nothing to do with card-playing. It is a habit which seems to grow on some people so much that it becomes at last a necessity, and they cannot live without it. "Madam," said Romaine to an old lady at Bath, who declared she could not do without her cards,—"Madam, if this is the case, cards are your god, and your god is a very poor one."

Surely in doubtful matters like these it is well to give our souls the benefit of the doubt, and to refrain.

(c) Concerning field-sports, I admit that it is not easy to lay down a strict rule. I cannot go the length of some, and say that galloping across country, or shooting grouse, partridges, or pheasants, or catching salmon or trout, are in themselves positively sinful occupations, and distinct marks of an unconverted heart. There are many persons, I know, to whom violent outdoor exercise and complete diversion of

mind are absolute necessities, for the preservation of their bodily and mental health. But in all these matters the chief question is one of degree.

Much depends on the company men are thrown into, and the extent to which the thing is carried. The great danger lies in excess. It is possible to be intemperate about hunting and shooting as well as about drinking. We are commanded in Scripture to be "temperate in all things," if we would so run as to obtain; and those who are addicted to field-sports should not forget this rule.

The question, however, is one about which Christians must be careful in expressing an opinion, and moderate in their judgments. The man who can neither ride, nor shoot, nor throw a fly, is hardly qualified to speak dispassionately about such matters. It is cheap and easy work to condemn others for doing things which you cannot do yourself, and are utterly unable to enjoy! One thing only is perfectly certain,— all intemperance or excess is sin. The man

J. C. Ryle

who is wholly absorbed in field-sports, and spends all his years in such a manner that he seems to think God only created him to be a "hunting, shooting, and fishing animal," is a man who at present knows very little of Scriptural Christianity. It is written, "Where your treasure is, there will your heart be also." (Matt. 6:21.)

Separation from the World

J. C. Ryle

Printed in Great Britain
by Amazon